THE TRUMP DERANGEMENT SYNDROME HANDBOOK

HOW TO SURVIVE MEDIA LIES, POLITICAL INSANITY, AND LIBERAL MELTDOWNS—AT HOME, WORK, AND ONLINE

LLOYD BECKMAN

ISBN: 978-1-958118-59-7| paperback

CONTENTS

THE TRUMP DERANGEMENT
SYNDROME HANDBOOK

To those who tried to cancel me—
You failed.

Your outrage only made this book happen. So really,
thank you.

Enjoy your soy lattes.

— Lloyd Beckman

INTRODUCTION

WELCOME TO THE MADNESS

Imagine waking up in the morning, brewing a fresh cup of coffee, and scrolling through the news, only to find that somewhere in America, another person has just lost their mind over Donald J. Trump. Not because he did anything in particular today—he might be golfing, eating a cheeseburger, or just minding his own business at Mar-a-Lago. But none of that matters, because the mere thought of Trump is enough to send certain individuals into a full-blown, foaming-at-the-mouth meltdown.

Ladies and gentlemen, welcome to Trump Derangement Syndrome (TDS).

You've seen it. You've heard it. Maybe you've even been on the receiving end of it. Perhaps you innocently mentioned that gas was cheaper in 2020, or you dared to suggest that maybe, just maybe, not everyone wearing a red hat is a literal Nazi. And just like that, a friend, coworker, or even your own mother lost their minds.

Fear not. This book is your survival guide.

~

WHAT IS TDS?

Trump Derangement Syndrome is an extreme emotional reaction to Donald Trump's mere existence. It's not just disliking the guy. It's not even disagreeing with his policies. It's a full-scale, irrational obsession where every single problem in the world is somehow traced back to him.

Think of it like an allergy. Some people sneeze when they encounter pollen; others start convulsing at the sight of a MAGA hat.

Some defining characteristics of TDS include:

- A visceral hatred of Trump, even for things he hasn't done.
- An obsession with MSNBC, CNN, and *The New York Times*, as if Rachel Maddow is their personal guru.
- An inability to accept economic statistics that disprove the narrative (Yes, Jim, the economy was doing well before COVID. No, that doesn't mean you have to cry at the dinner table).
- Sudden hostility toward friends and family who fail to denounce Trump every 30 minutes.

The irony? Many TDS sufferers call Trump a narcissist—yet they spend more time thinking about him than his own supporters do.

Symptoms of TDS

TDS manifests in stages. Some cases are mild, while others are full-scale Hollywood-level meltdowns. Below is a handy guide to help you diagnose the afflicted:

Stage 1: Mild Annoyance

- Rolls eyes when Trump's name is mentioned.
- Complains about his "mean tweets."
- Insists they "used to be Republican" before Trump ruined everything.
- Uses the phrase, "I just wish we had a normal president again."

Prognosis: Annoying but manageable. With the right intervention (turning off CNN), recovery is possible.

Stage 2: Moderate Obsession

- Genuinely believes democracy is over if Trump orders a cheeseburger.
- Screams "HE'S A DICTATOR" while he's being impeached. (For the second time.)
- Thinks the Supreme Court, the economy, and the weather itself are all under Trump's secret control.

- Believes every protestor at the Capitol was personally invited by Trump via carrier pigeon.

Prognosis: Risky. They are too deep into the MSNBC vortex to be reasoned with, but not beyond hope. Recommend exposure to actual history books and a break from Twitter.

Stage 3: Full-Blown Hysteria

- Has physiological reactions to the color red.
- Sees Trump's face in their morning toast and takes it as a sign that America is doomed.
- Literally screamed at the sky when he won in 2016.
- Continues screaming at the sky in 2025.

Prognosis: Terminal. These individuals are beyond help. The best you can do is back away slowly and let them rant themselves into exhaustion.

Why This Book Exists

We are living in unprecedented times. Never before in history have we seen so many people completely unhinged over a single human being. It's almost impressive.

You might think, "But I'm not political. Why should I care?"

Oh, my sweet summer child. You don't have to be political

to become a target. Simply existing in the same space as a TDS sufferer is enough to trigger an episode.

- Mention gas prices? Boom. Argument.
- Wear an American flag pin? Boom. Meltdown.
- Say you don't watch *The View*? BOOM. Friendship over.

This book is here to help you navigate these interactions without losing your mind.

What can you expect?

✔ Tactics for surviving Thanksgiving dinner without being disowned.

✔ How to identify TDS in the wild—before it's too late.

✔ Techniques for dealing with "woke" coworkers who mistake Slack for a political debate club.

✔ Social media strategies that prevent you from engaging in pointless battles with people who have too much time on their hands.

And most importantly...

✔ How to laugh at the madness instead of getting sucked into it.

Disclaimer:

No, we are not doctors. But let's be honest—you don't need a PhD to spot crazy.

Key Takeaways

1. TDS is real, and it's hilarious to observe. (Yes, we should be concerned for democracy, but let's be honest—watching someone scream at a Starbucks employee because they forgot their oat milk *and* because "Trump destroyed America" is objectively funny.)

2. You are not alone—millions suffer due to friends and family with TDS. (We should form a support group.)

3. This book will teach you coping strategies for dealing with the afflicted. (Like nodding, smiling, and pretending to get a phone call whenever politics come up.)

4. Humor is your greatest weapon. (Sure, you could argue. But watching them self-destruct over a Tucker Carlson segment is way more entertaining.)

5. You cannot reason with full-blown TDS sufferers, but you can survive them. (Your best option? Step away, grab some popcorn, and let them rant themselves into exhaustion.)

～

Final Thoughts Before We Begin

If you've made it this far, congratulations!

You've already demonstrated more critical thinking skills than the average CNN panelist.

Now, let's begin your training in TDS survival tactics. By the time you finish this book, you'll know how to handle your hysterical coworkers, survive holiday gatherings, and escape social media debates unscathed.

More importantly?

You'll know how to laugh at the madness.

Because at the end of the day...

You can't fix crazy. But you can definitely enjoy the show.

Now, turn the page and let's dive into the insanity.

"To argue with a man who has renounced the use and authority of reason, and whose philosophy consists in holding humanity in contempt, is like administering medicine to the dead."

— THOMAS PAINE

THE STAGES OF TDS – FROM MILD DISCOMFORT TO FULL-BLOWN HYSTERIA

I f you've ever made the grave mistake of mentioning that you think the economy was doing pretty well a few years ago—only to witness a friend, coworker, or family member erupt into a frothing rage—congratulations. You've encountered Trump Derangement Syndrome in the wild.

But here's the thing: Not all cases of TDS are the same.

Like a progressive illness, TDS manifests in stages, ranging from mild irritation to full-scale hysteria. Some cases can be managed with logic, patience, and limited exposure to Twitter, while others? Well... some folks are beyond saving.

To help you navigate the madness, I've categorized TDS into three levels of severity: Mild, Moderate, and Severe. Think of this as a medical diagnostic tool—except instead of checking for symptoms like fever and fatigue, we're looking for signs like irrational hatred of tax cuts and spontaneous rage at red hats.

THE MILD CASE

The mildest form of TDS is relatively harmless—think of it like a seasonal allergy. It flares up occasionally, but with proper treatment (avoiding cable news and excessive Twitter usage), there's a chance of recovery.

Symptoms of Mild TDS:

- Occasional rants about "mean tweets."
- "I just wish he wasn't so RUDE!" (sips pumpkin spice latte aggressively)
- "Why does he have to insult people all the time?" (scrolls through 17 Joy Reid tweets insulting conservatives)
- "Can't we have a NORMAL president again?" (forgets about Bill Clinton's office behavior and Obama's drone strikes)
- Gets visibly irritated when hearing the word "MAGA."
- "Ugh, that slogan is SO stupid. America was never NOT great!"
- Accidentally wears a red hat to a baseball game, gets side-eyed by strangers.
- "MAGA people just don't understand how things REALLY work!" (has never run a business, signed a paycheck, or left a major city)
- Thinks Trump supporters are just "misguided."
- "I don't HATE them... I just think they're brainwashed by Fox News."

- "If they read *The New York Times*, they'd see the truth!"
- "Trump voters are mostly just uneducated." (ignores Trump's gains with minorities and working-class voters)

Prognosis:

- Good chance of recovery—Mild TDS sufferers can sometimes be cured by forcing them to spend one week away from social media.
- Treatment options: Introduce them to alternative news sources, common sense, and economic data. Proceed with caution—too much reality at once may cause cognitive dissonance.

THE MODERATE CASE

At this stage, the sufferer is fully immersed in the belief that Trump is responsible for every bad thing that has ever happened. Their worldview is shaped not by facts, but by whatever the latest MSNBC chyron tells them to believe.

Logic? Irrelevant.

Facts? Problematic.

Common sense? Bigotry.

Symptoms of Moderate TDS:

- Believes Trump controls hurricanes and wildfires.

- "That hurricane? TRUMP CAUSED IT with CLIMATE DENIAL."
- "Trump is literally setting forests on fire by rolling back regulations!"
- Never questions why California wildfires happen every year under Democrat governors.
- Thinks Trump is "literally Putin's puppet" despite zero evidence.
- "He COLLUDES with Russia! I saw it on Maddow!"
- "Mueller is COMING FOR HIM!" (Mueller finds nothing) "That just proves how deep the cover-up goes!"
- "Trump is working for the Kremlin!" (Ignores that Russia invaded Ukraine under Biden, not Trump)
- Would rather drink expired oat milk than admit Trump did anything good.
- "Lowest unemployment ever? Well, OBAMA set that up!"
- "Peace deals in the Middle East? Doesn't count!"
- "The economy was booming? But at what cost?!" (Can't explain what that cost is)

Prognosis:

- Moderate cases require patience. You CAN still reason with them—but only in small doses.
- Treatment options: Exposure therapy—force them to read an article NOT written by *The Atlantic*.

- **Warning**: If confronted with reality too quickly, they may accuse you of spreading Russian disinformation.

THE SEVERE CASE

At this point, the sufferer has lost all grip on reality. They have built their entire personality around hating Trump, and even his removal from office has not alleviated their suffering.

Symptoms of Severe TDS:

- Sees "Trump" hidden in every bad thing (gas prices, global warming, their own weight gain).
- "GAS PRICES ARE HIGH BECAUSE OF TRUMP'S POLICIES!" (Even though he was out of office for years)
- "COVID was his fault!" (Despite Biden catching it multiple times)
- "I gained 15 pounds? STRESS FROM TRUMP!" (Ignores daily Starbucks runs and lack of exercise)
- Believes Trump's removal from office is the only path to inner peace.
- "My depression will end when Trump is in jail!" (Trump is still free, they are still depressed)
- "America CAN'T HEAL until we erase his existence!"
- Finds a MAGA hat in Goodwill, burns it in an exorcism-style ritual.
- "Even though he's gone, he's still ruining my life!"

- "TRUMPISM is still here! And it's WORSE!"
- "Anyone who voted for him is just as bad!"
- "We need to put all Trump voters on a watchlist!"

Prognosis:

- Terminal.
- There is NO reasoning with a severe TDS sufferer.
- Your best option? RUN.

Key Takeaways

1. TDS exists in stages, much like a progressive illness. (Some start off mildly annoyed; others end up shrieking in the streets.)

2. The mild cases can sometimes be cured with logic. (But go slow—too much reality at once may cause short-circuiting.)

3. The moderate cases require patience, but there's hope. (They still live in an MSNBC bubble, but light exposure to facts might help.)

4. The severe cases? RUN. (These people are too far gone. No amount of logic, therapy, or Biden-flavored ice cream will save them.)

5.Treat them like emotional toddlers—do not engage in their tantrums. (You wouldn't argue with a screaming three-year-old in a supermarket, would you? Same principle applies here.)

~

Final Thoughts

If you find yourself interacting with a mild to moderate TDS sufferer, there's a chance you can bring them back to reality. But if you're dealing with a full-blown, severe case, accept the inevitable: They will never, ever, ever stop talking about Trump. Not today. Not tomorrow. Not even in 2035.

Your best bet? Laugh at the madness, walk away when necessary, and always keep an emergency escape plan for Thanksgiving dinner.

Because if we've learned anything over the last few years, it's this:

You can't fix crazy.

But you CAN survive it.

2

THE SCIENCE (OR LACK THEREOF) BEHIND TDS

I f you've ever witnessed a grown adult react to the word "Trump" the way a vampire reacts to sunlight, you might have asked yourself:

"Is there some kind of medical explanation for this?"

It's a fair question.

Trump Derangement Syndrome is one of the most bizarre psychological phenomena of our time. We've seen normally rational people—neighbors, teachers, relatives who once seemed perfectly fine—descend into a state of constant hysteria, paranoia, and foaming rage over one man.

So, is TDS an actual neurological disorder? A media-induced psychosis? Or just the world's longest tantrum?

Let's examine the science (or lack thereof) behind this phenomenon.

Is TDS a Neurological Disorder?

Scientists haven't *officially* classified TDS in the *Diagnostic and Statistical Manual of Mental Disorders* (DSM-5) yet, but let's be honest—they probably should.

If psychologists can create a term like "Oppositional Defiant Disorder" (which basically means your kid doesn't listen), then surely a condition that causes adults to scream at the sky should warrant at least a footnote in medical literature.

What Would an MRI Scan of a TDS Sufferer Show?

We don't have official brain scans of TDS patients (yet), but if we did, the results would probably look something like this:

- Significant anxiety spikes when hearing the name "Trump."
- Overactivity in the rage-processing centers of the brain, particularly when exposed to photos of red hats.
- Diminished critical thinking ability when confronted with actual economic data.

In layman's terms: It's not a logical condition—it's an *emotional* one.

THE PHYSIOLOGICAL REACTIONS OF TDS SUFFERERS

TDS doesn't just exist in the mind—it manifests physically. Watch for these telltale signs of distress:

- Elevated heart rate when hearing Trump speak.
- Involuntary eye twitching at the sight of a MAGA rally.
- Shortness of breath and hand-waving when discussing the Electoral College.
- Shaking and hyperventilating at the mention of the Supreme Court.
- In severe cases, sufferers may experience:
- Spontaneous, uncontrollable Twitter rants.
- A compulsion to protest outside courthouses in inflatable T-Rex suits.
- An inability to function unless Trump is actively being investigated for something.

WHY ISN'T THERE AN OFFICIAL CURE?

Because political derangement is a deeply emotional condition, not a logical one.

Imagine trying to "cure" a toddler mid-tantrum by explaining tax policy—it's not going to work. The key is emotional regulation, which, unfortunately, many sufferers seem to have outsourced to MSNBC.

CAN TDS BE CURED?

Good news: Some people recover from TDS.

Bad news: Others stay permanently lost in a dystopian fever dream.

Spontaneous Recovery: It Happens!

Much like a fever that finally breaks, some sufferers snap out of it after an unexpected "Red Pill" moment.

Common Triggers for Spontaneous Recovery:

Realizing their taxes were lower under Trump.

- "Wait a minute... I used to get a better refund!"
- Checks pay stub.
- Starts questioning everything they've ever been told.

Noticing that their 401(k) looked a lot healthier pre-2021.

- "Why was my retirement account growing before, but now it's tanking?"
- "Why does it cost $11 for eggs?"
- Has a quiet existential crisis in the grocery store.
- Seeing the media contradict themselves.
- "So wait, we're mad about *this* now? But I thought *that* was good last year..."
- Finally realizes that cable news is just outrage theater.

The Role of Cognitive Dissonance

For some, TDS recovery is painful.

- They want to believe Trump is the root of all evil, but...
- They can't deny that their quality of life was better before.

This creates cognitive dissonance—that uncomfortable mental friction when reality contradicts deeply held beliefs (MSEd, 2025). Some choose to face the truth; others double down and blame Trump for things he had nothing to do with.

High-Risk Individuals: Who Is Most Likely to Stay Stuck?

Some people are more susceptible to TDS than others.

High-risk factors include:

Excessive exposure to corporate media.

- Watching CNN for more than 3 hours per day is known to cause long-term damage.
- Symptoms include repeating phrases like "threat to democracy" and "Orange Hitler."

Belief in elaborate anti-Trump conspiracy theories.

- "Trump is controlling the government from Mar-a-Lago!"
- "The Supreme Court is just a front for Trump's secret army!"
- "He's actually Putin's top agent—despite sanctioning Russia more than Obama did."

A tendency to blame external forces for personal unhappiness.

- "I didn't get that job because of TRUMP!"
- "My boyfriend dumped me—IT'S TRUMP'S FAULT!"
- "I burned my toast—CLEARLY TRUMP'S DOING!"

THE ROLE OF SOCIAL MEDIA IN FUELING TDS

Much like a petri dish growing bacteria, TDS thrives in the perfect environment: social media echo chambers.

How Social Media Worsens Symptoms

Outrage = Engagement

- Platforms prioritize outrage-inducing content because it keeps people addicted.
- The angrier someone gets, the more they post, share, and argue—feeding the machine.

The Algorithm Spiral

- You watch one video about how Trump is destroying democracy...
- YouTube suggests 50 more just like it...
- Two weeks later, you're convinced he controls the weather.

MSNBC & CNN: The 24/7 Panic Machine

- "Tonight at 7: Why Trump is still secretly in power!"
- "Breaking: Trump's Diet Coke order PROVES he's planning a coup!"
- "Exclusive: Anonymous sources claim Trump is hiding in your closet!"

Step One to Recovery? TURN OFF THE TV.

- No, really. Turn it off.
- If you know someone suffering from TDS, stage an intervention and cancel their cable subscription.
- They may resist at first, but after 48 hours of fresh air, they might start thinking clearly again.

KEY TAKEAWAYS

1. TDS isn't officially a disorder, but we all know it should be. (Some people need a "12-step program" for quitting MSNBC cold turkey.)

2. Some recover once removed from the social media outrage machine. (The first step is admitting you have a problem—and deleting Twitter.)

3. The media profits from keeping people in a state of hysteria. (If their viewers calm down, they go out of business.)

4. Echo chambers worsen symptoms—limit exposure. (Your crazy uncle isn't crazy—he's just overdosed on CNN.)

5. Turning off CNN is an essential first step to healing. (Unplug, go outside, and touch some grass. It's good for you.)

Suggested Resources

The Coddling of the American Mind – Jonathan Haidt (Why outrage culture thrives).

The Madness of Crowds – Douglas Murray (On mass hysteria in modern culture).

~

FINAL THOUGHTS

TDS might not be an official disease, but we all know it's real.

The good news? It's possible to recover.

The bad news? Some people don't want to.

Your best bet? Step away, laugh at the madness, and never, ever engage in a Twitter debate.

3

HOW TO IDENTIFY TDS IN THE WILD

TDS sufferers are not rare creatures. You don't have to go on a special safari to find them—you can encounter them in the grocery store, at work, at Thanksgiving dinner, or even in your own family group chat (assuming you haven't been blocked yet).

But how do you spot a TDS sufferer before it's too late? How can you tell if the person in front of you is just a mildly opinionated liberal or a full-blown, red-hat-phobic hysteric?

In this chapter, we'll explore how to identify TDS in the wild, the common phrases and behaviors to look for, and even a quiz to test if your friend, family member, or coworker is afflicted.

Let's begin your TDS Identification Training.

COMMON PHRASES: HOW TDS SUFFERERS COMMUNICATE

TDS sufferers tend to speak in slogans rather than logic. Their arguments are not based on facts, policies, or historical context—they are pure emotion, regurgitated from Twitter soundbites.

Here are some of the most common phrases you'll hear from a TDS sufferer:

Democracy is over!

Translation: "I didn't like the outcome of an election!"

Reality check: If democracy were truly over, you wouldn't be tweeting about it from a Starbucks while sipping a $7 oat milk latte.

- TDS sufferers love to claim democracy is collapsing—yet strangely, they never seem to be silenced.
- They will shout "fascism" while posting freely on Twitter and TikTok, never realizing the irony.
- Ask them to define democracy—watch them struggle.

He's literally a dictator!

Translation: "I don't know what a dictator actually is!"

Reality check:

- If Trump were a dictator, he wouldn't have been impeached twice.
- Dictators don't allow constant protests, late-night comedians mocking them, and social media outrage mobs.
- Ask them if they think Kim Jong-Un, Stalin, or Hitler were also voted out of office. (Watch their brain short-circuit.)

I just CAN'T with these MAGA people!

Translation: "I have no arguments, so I will declare emotional exhaustion instead!"

Reality check:

- This phrase is used when a TDS sufferer realizes they cannot win an argument.
- It's a defensive mechanism—instead of debating, they just "CAN'T EVEN."
- If you hear this phrase, congratulations—you have exceeded their logic capacity.

TELLTALE SIGNS OF TDS IN THE WILD

Sometimes, you don't even need to hear them speak—TDS sufferers exhibit clear physical and behavioral symptoms when triggered.

1. Hyperventilates at the mention of "Trump 2024."

- Casual mentions of Trump's comeback can cause immediate distress.
- Signs to look for: Sudden sweating, hand-wringing, frantic Google searches for "how to move to Canada."
- Extreme cases: May need to be placed in a safe space with a weighted blanket and soothing whale sounds.

2. Develops Physical Tics Upon Hearing Sean Hannity's Voice.

Hannity, Tucker Carlson, Ben Shapiro—anyone outside the MSNBC bubble—causes involuntary eye twitching.

If forced to listen, they may exhibit:

- Clenching their fists.
- Shouting "PROPAGANDA!" at inanimate objects.
- Googling "How to report a hate crime" with shaking hands.

3. Uses "Fascist" for Anyone Who Disagrees with Them.

In their world, a fascist is literally anyone with a different opinion.

The bar for fascism keeps getting lower:

- Voted Republican? Fascist.
- Supports free speech? Fascist.
- Ordered Chick-fil-A? Ultra-mega-fascist.

∼

QUIZ: Does Your Friend Have TDS?

It's time for a scientific (loosely speaking) assessment. Answer the following questions and calculate their TDS score.

1. Do they blame Trump for things that happened AFTER he left office?

A. No, they understand time and causality. (0 points)
B. Sometimes, if it fits their narrative. (2 points)
C. Absolutely—Trump is responsible for gas prices, inflation, and the war in Ukraine. (3 points)

2. Have they rage-unfriended family members over politics?

A. No, they value relationships over political drama. (o points)
B. Yes, but only distant cousins. (2 points)
C. Yes, including their own mother. (3 points)

3. Do they consume 8+ hours of political content per day?

A. No, they have other hobbies. (o points)
B. Yes, but they watch a mix of viewpoints. (2 points)
C. Yes, exclusively MSNBC, CNN, and Twitter arguments. (3 points)

4. Have they ever screamed in public about Trump?

A. No, that would be ridiculous. (o points)
B. Once, at a protest. (2 points)
C. Yes, multiple times—including in restaurants, weddings, and yoga class. (3 points)

5. Do they believe Trump is still secretly running the government from Mar-a-Lago?

A. No, that's absurd. (o points)
B. They're suspicious but can't prove it. (2 points)
C. Yes, and they have a conspiracy theory thread to prove it. (3 points)

Results:

0–2 points
Safe Zone – Your friend is mostly sane. Proceed as usual.

3–5 points
Proceed with Caution – They show mild TDS symptoms. Avoid political discussions.

6+ points
RUN! – You are dealing with a full-blown TDS sufferer. Do NOT engage. Exit the conversation immediately!

KEY TAKEAWAYS

1. TDS sufferers speak in slogans, not facts. ("Democracy is over!" "Trump is a dictator!"—it's all soundbites, no substance.)

2. They exhibit physical distress at the mention of Trump. (Heart rate spikes, hyperventilation, and aggressive oat milk consumption may occur.)

3. Self-awareness is low—they don't realize they sound crazy. (To them, calling their cousin a Nazi over tax policy is completely reasonable.)

4. TDS manifests both online and offline—avoid prolonged exposure. (Social media is a breeding ground for TDS. Too much Twitter = brain rot.)

5. If someone starts frothing at the mouth over a red hat, it's time to walk away. (Your sanity is more important than winning an argument.)

~

FINAL THOUGHTS

Identifying TDS in the wild is an essential survival skill. By learning the phrases, behaviors, and warning signs, you can avoid unnecessary confrontations, protect your sanity, and—most importantly—enjoy watching the madness unfold from a safe distance.

Because remember: You can't reason with crazy.

But you CAN avoid it.

Now, let's move on to Chapter 4, where we'll teach you how to survive TDS during family gatherings—without flipping the dinner table.

4

DEALING WITH TDS AT THE THANKSGIVING TABLE

A h, Thanksgiving—a time for gratitude, turkey, family bonding, and... political combat zones.

For most people, Thanksgiving is a time to stuff their faces and enjoy mild family dysfunction. But if you have a TDS-afflicted relative, the holiday takes on a different tone. You are now walking into a minefield where the wrong comment—or even just breathing in the wrong direction—can set off an emotional meltdown of historic proportions.

Fear not.

This chapter will prepare you for battle. You will learn:

✔ How to navigate Thanksgiving without losing your mind

✔ How to avoid political ambushes from your blue-haired aunt

✔ Escape strategies that guarantee your survival (and maybe even some extra pie)

Because let's be honest—no one has ever changed their political views over stuffing.

HOW TO SURVIVE HOLIDAY DINNERS WITHOUT A FULL-BLOWN POLITICAL MELTDOWN

Step 1: Accept That Politics Will Come Up – Prepare Yourself for an Ambush

Before you even step foot into the dining room, understand this:

- Politics WILL be brought up.
- It will be framed as an "innocent discussion."
- It is, in fact, a trap.

Scenario:

You're calmly passing the mashed potatoes when suddenly, your cousin Karen with the blue hair turns to you with a smug grin and asks:

Soooo, are you still supporting that orange fascist?

Your uncle Jeff, who has been waiting for this moment all year, leans in.

Suddenly, all eyes are on you.

What do you do?

- Option 1: Engage and Fight – (Not recommended unless you enjoy watching Grandma clutch her pearls in horror.)
- Option 2: Deflect and Escape – (Best option—more on this soon.)
- Option 3: Pretend You Didn't Hear It – ("What? Sorry, I was just thinking about how delicious this stuffing is.")

Step 2: Identify the Most Unhinged Family Member – They Will Lead the Charge

Every family has one.

The person who watches Rachel Maddow religiously, has an "In This House, We Believe" sign on their lawn, and believes Trump is secretly controlling the government from his golf cart.

Signs you've found them:

- They refer to Jan 6th as "Worse than 9/11."
- They have a "Not My President" bumper sticker.
- They refer to anyone right of Bernie Sanders as a "literal fascist."
- Their personal identity is 50% astrology and 50% blaming Trump for things he had nothing to do with.

Your strategy: Avoid them at all costs.

Do not engage.

If cornered, divert their energy toward someone else:

- "Oh wow, Aunt Carol, did you hear that Uncle Dave actually voted for a third-party candidate? Crazy, right?"
- "Didn't Grandma say something pro-capitalism the other day?"

BOOM.

Suddenly, you're in the clear, and the fireworks move elsewhere.

Step 3: Have Pre-Planned Exit Strategies

A skilled survivor always has an escape plan.

Here are some guaranteed ways to exit a heated political discussion before it spirals:

Fake a phone call.
"Oh wow, sorry, I need to take this—it's my friend who got stuck in a debate about the Electoral College and needs saving."

Pretend the turkey is burning.
"Oh my gosh! The turkey—does anyone smell smoke?!"
(Even if the turkey is fine, panic and run to the kitchen. They'll be too busy arguing about climate change to check.)

Claim indigestion.
"Ugh, too much gravy, I need a minute."
(A bonus: This allows you to retreat to the bathroom for as long as necessary.)

Remember: A swift, graceful exit is key to preserving your sanity.

THE ART OF DEFLECTION: CHANGING THE SUBJECT

If you can't escape, you need to redirect the conversation.

Safe Topics to Change the Subject

- Sports – "Can you believe that last game?" (But avoid kneeling conversations!)
- Movies & TV – "Did you see the new season of Yellowstone?" (Avoid *The Handmaid's Tale*—it's a TDS trigger!)
- Weather – "Crazy how warm it's been, huh?" (Careful—they might blame Trump for hurricanes!)

If Cornered, Use Neutral Responses

Sometimes, you can't avoid a direct question. Instead of arguing, use non-committal phrases that confuse them long enough for you to escape.

- "That's interesting." (Doesn't mean you agree, doesn't mean you don't.)
- "I see your point." (Even if you don't.)

- "Huh. Wild times we're living in." (Works every time.)

Advanced Level: The Master Pivot

- If the conversation turns into a trap, quickly change the subject.
- Example: "Hey, did anyone see Grandma's stuffing recipe?! I NEED that in my life."
- Watch as they instantly forget about Trump and start talking about food.

ESCAPE STRATEGIES: HOW TO LEAVE WITHOUT CAUSING A SCENE

Sometimes, no amount of deflection will save you. In that case, you need a fast and effective exit.

Option 1: The Bathroom Emergency

- Success Rate: 100%
- *Oh wow, I need the restroom real quick—be right back.*
- **Pro tip**: Stay in there long enough for the conversation to shift.

Option 2: Pretend to Be Extremely Focused on the Food

- Success Rate: 85%
- *This cranberry sauce has such a unique flavor— what's the secret ingredient?!*
- Watch as the conversation suddenly turns into a food debate instead.

Option 3: Use a Child or Pet as a Distraction

- Success Rate: 90%
- *Look, Timmy just put mashed potatoes in his ears!*
- *Where's the dog? Let's go find him!*

Children and pets are nature's built-in distraction devices. Use them wisely.

KEY TAKEAWAYS

1. Thanksgiving should be about turkey, not tantrums. (Nobody came here for a debate on the Electoral College.)

2. Never engage a full-blown TDS sufferer unless you enjoy public spectacles. (Do you really want to be screamed at over sweet potatoes? Didn't think so.)

3. Mastering the art of deflection is key. (A well-timed food question can save you from a political ambush.)

4. If things get too heated, walk away with dignity (and extra pie). (Make your escape before things spiral into a full-fledged Twitter thread.)

5. No one has ever changed their political views over stuffing. (Save yourself the headache. Just nod, smile, and eat more mashed potatoes.)

∾

FINAL THOUGHTS

Thanksgiving is supposed to be a joyful occasion—not a cage match between you and your activist cousin.

By using these tactics, deflections, and escape routes, you'll make it through the meal unscathed and still be invited back next year.

Because at the end of the day...

Pumpkin pie > Political arguments.

Now, let's move on to "Chapter 5: The Workplace Survival Guide"—because surviving family arguments is one thing, but dealing with woke coworkers?

That's a whole new challenge.

5

THE WORKPLACE SURVIVAL GUIDE

Welcome to the corporate battlefield, where productivity takes a backseat to performative wokeness, and the biggest risk to your career isn't missing a deadline—it's accidentally saying something reasonable in front of the wrong coworker.

Once upon a time, workplaces were for working—not for debating social justice theories, complaining about democracy, or insisting that not using someone's preferred pronouns is literal violence.

But today? The modern office is a political minefield.

This chapter will teach you:

✔ How to navigate work without getting dragged into ideological debates
✔ How to handle woke coworkers without setting off an HR alarm

✔ The art of corporate code-switching so you can survive without compromising your sanity

Because let's be real—if HR gets involved, you've already lost.

How to Handle Woke Coworkers Without Getting HR Complaints

First things first—your workplace is NOT a safe space (for political sanity, at least).

This is enemy territory. You need to move carefully, like a CIA agent deep undercover. The key is to avoid triggering anyone's delicate sensibilities while also not losing your own mind.

Step 1: Keep Politics Out of the Break Room – That's What Twitter is For

There was a time when break room conversations revolved around harmless topics like:

- How awful Mondays are.
- What Karen from accounting did at the company happy hour.
- Whether *The Office* is still funny on the 7th rewatch.

But now? One wrong word and you're in an impromptu social justice seminar.

BREAK ROOM DANGER SIGNS

- Your coworker asks, "Did you see that article about white supremacy in office culture?"
- Someone refers to January 6th as "the darkest day in American history."
- You hear the phrase "late-stage capitalism" from a guy who just ordered DoorDash for the 3rd time today.

Step 2: Learn the "Nod and Smile Method" – It Works Wonders

The Nod and Smile Method is your best defense.

- It creates the illusion of engagement without requiring actual agreement.
- It neutralizes aggressive activists before they try to recruit you.
- It lets you escape conversations unscathed.

Examples of proper execution:

Coworker: "Trump is literally a dictator."
You: Nod... smile... take a sip of coffee... walk away.

Coworker: "I just CAN'T with conservatives anymore."
You: "Huh... yeah, wild times." (Then fake a phone call.)

Coworker: "Do you agree that anyone who doesn't support equity policies is a white supremacist?"
You: "That's interesting." (Adds more sugar to coffee as an escape tactic.)

Pro tip: If all else fails, pretend to receive an urgent email and dramatically walk away.

Step 3: If Someone Asks for Your Opinion, Redirect

There's always that one coworker who insists on dragging you into political conversations.

To avoid becoming a workplace pariah, master the art of the redirect.

Situation: A coworker asks, "What do you think about the latest Trump indictment?"

- Wrong Answer: "It's a political witch hunt." (Congrats, you've just been reported to HR!)
- Right Answer: "I try to stay out of politics—how's your project going?" (Perfect dodge!)

Other useful redirects:

- "Man, I'm just trying to get through my inbox."
- "I don't really follow politics. What did you think of last night's game?"

- "I haven't had my coffee yet—brain's not working."

Remember: Refusing to engage is NOT agreement. It's self-preservation.

CODE-SWITCHING TECHNIQUES: SPEAKING IN CORPORATE JARGON TO AVOID DETECTION

Sometimes, you're forced to say something—but you can't say what you really mean.

That's where corporate code-switching comes in.

Here's how to translate normal thoughts into workplace-safe jargon:

> Instead of saying: "That's insane."
> Say: "That's an interesting perspective."
>
> Instead of saying: "That makes no sense."
> Say: "I see how you came to that conclusion."
>
> Instead of saying: *"You're completely wrong."
> Say: "I think we're looking at this from different angles."
>
> Instead of saying: "That's dumb."
> Say: "That's certainly one way to look at it."

This neutral corporate language allows you to disengage

without offending anyone, protecting you from HR while maintaining your sanity.

WHEN TO ENGAGE VS. WHEN TO NOD AND SIP YOUR COFFEE

Not all workplace discussions are landmines—but some should be avoided at all costs.

Engage if: It's a rational discussion with a normal person

- You actually respect the person you're talking to.
- They don't foam at the mouth when you mention free speech.
- There's mutual respect, and you can debate without getting canceled.

Avoid if: They start sentences with "as a person of..."

> **Warning**: If someone starts a sentence with "As a person of..." you are about to enter a no-win situation.

- "As a woman..."
- "As a queer, non-binary, pansexual neurodivergent person..."
- "As a member of the oppressed working class..."

Exit immediately.

Nod and sip coffee if they bring up Trump while discussing printer paper shortages.

- "I can't believe we're out of printer paper... thanks, Trump."
- "Why is it so cold in here? Late-stage capitalism and Trump's climate policies, probably."
- "This vending machine price hike is another sign of MAGA fascism!"

Nod. Smile. Take a sip of coffee. Do **NOT** engage.

Key Takeaways

1. Work is for working—not political battles. (You are not paid to debate Karl Marx vs. Adam Smith in the break room.)

2. The nod and smile strategy prevents unnecessary drama. (Master this move, and you'll avoid 99% of workplace conflicts.)

3. Corporate speak is your best defense against workplace radicals. ("I see your point" = The magic words that make you untouchable.)

4. If HR is involved, you've already lost—retreat immediately. (Do not pass Go, do not collect $200, and definitely do not try to reason with them.)

5. Don't bring a MAGA mug unless you enjoy office riots. (Your coworker wearing a "Tax the Rich" hoodie might throw a stapler at you.)

Suggested Resources

📖 *How to Work with Stupid People* – JS Paxton (Your workplace survival guide.)

∼

FINAL THOUGHTS

Navigating a woke workplace is a delicate dance. The goal is not to get fired while also not losing your sanity.

By keeping politics out of work, deflecting wisely, and mastering corporate jargon, you can survive the modern office without turning into a social justice casualty.

Now, let's move on to "Chapter 6: TDS on Social Media – A No-Win Battlefield." Because if you thought the workplace was bad... wait until you see what happens online.

6

TDS ON SOCIAL MEDIA – A NO-WIN BATTLEFIELD

If Thanksgiving dinner is where TDS sufferers first train for combat, social media is where they take their skills to the Olympic level.

Welcome to the digital coliseum, where outrage is currency, facts are optional, and every minor inconvenience is somehow Trump's fault.

Social media should be a place to share dog pictures, post vacation selfies, and keep up with old high school friends. Instead, it has become a screaming match between the perpetually offended and those who dare to have a different opinion.

And you—a rational, sane human being—might be tempted to step in and restore logic to the world.

DON'T.

This chapter will teach you:

> ✔ Why engaging in social media arguments is a losing battle
> ✔ How to identify different species of TDS sufferers online
> ✔ The best tactics for responding (or escaping) without losing your mind

Because at the end of the day, you're not going to change anyone's mind in a Facebook thread.

AVOIDING THE BAIT – THE INTERNET IS **NOT** WHERE ARGUMENTS ARE WON

Engaging with TDS sufferers online is like arguing with a parrot that only knows three phrases:

- "Trump is literally Hitler!"
- "This is a THREAT to democracy!"
- "If you support him, you're a fascist!"

There is no winning. There is no reasoning. There is only wasted time and rising blood pressure.

Before you even think about engaging, memorize these three golden rules:

Rule #1: You Will Never Change Someone's Mind in a Facebook Thread.

Reality check:

- Nobody has ever read a Facebook argument and thought, "Wow, I see your point! I've been wrong all along."
- What actually happens? People dig in deeper, convinced that they're fighting for justice and democracy instead of just arguing with a stranger in their pajamas.
- TDS sufferers don't come to social media for debate. They come for validation.

Best strategy: DON'T ENGAGE.

Rule #2: The Longer the Comment, the More Irrational the Person.

Warning signs:

- Their comment is longer than the U.S. Constitution.
- It contains footnotes, a 17-point argument, and five links to CNN articles.
- It reads like a manifesto, complete with words in all caps for emphasis.

Best strategy: If you see a novel-length comment, just walk away.

(If you feel the urge to respond, go touch some grass instead.)

Rule #3: No One Reads Past the Second Sentence—Keep Scrolling.

Social media truths:

- Most people don't even read articles before commenting (which explains a lot).
- If your response isn't a meme or a GIF, it's too long.
- If you must say something, keep it under five words—preferably one.

Best strategy: Say less. Scroll more. Live longer.

Types of TDS Sufferers Online

Much like wildlife biologists categorize different species, we can classify TDS sufferers into specific digital subspecies.

Below are the most common types you will encounter:

1. The Caps Lock Warrior

Battle cry: "THIS IS LITERALLY FASCISM!!!!"

Defining characteristics:

- EVERYTHING IS IN ALL CAPS.
- Ends every sentence with multiple exclamation marks and sometimes a crying emoji.
- Believes anyone who disagrees with them is an "actual Nazi."

Best response?

- The "Haha" React (More on this later.)
- No words—just let them scream into the void.

2. The #Resistance Meme Lord

Battle cry: "Orange Man Bad."

Defining characteristics:

- Posts terrible political memes that don't make sense.
- Still thinks "Covfefe" is the height of comedy (even though it happened years ago).
- Believes Twitter activists are real-life heroes.

Best response?

- A better meme (but do you really want to waste your time?).
- Let them live in their delusional digital safe space.

3. The "I Used to Be a Republican, But..." Guy

Battle cry: "I LOVED Reagan, but Trump RUINED conservatism!"

Defining characteristics:

- Loves telling you they were a Republican once (back when Eisenhower was president).

- Thinks Lincoln would have voted for Hillary.
- Always conveniently appears in every political thread, like a digital NPC.

Best response?

- "Cool story, bro."
- Move along—this guy never actually voted Republican.

How to Respond Without Losing Your Mind (or Getting Banned)

Since some interactions are unavoidable, here are the best strategies to survive online debates without ending up in Facebook jail.

1. The "Haha" React Strategy – Respond with Laughter Instead of Rage

Why it works:

- TDS sufferers want to make you mad.
- When you just laugh at them, it destroys their argument instantly.
- It signals to others that you're not taking them seriously.

Example:

> TDS sufferer: "Trump is literally a dictator!"
> You: 😂
>
> TDS sufferer: "This is a THREAT to democracy!"
> You: 😂😂😂

(Watch them spiral into an even bigger meltdown—without you even saying a word!)

2. The One-Word Response – "Interesting" or "Huh."

Why it works:

- It leaves them frustrated and confused.
- It kills the argument without engaging in one.

Example:

> TDS sufferer: "Trump is destroying America!!"
> You: "Interesting."
>
> TDS sufferer: "He's a Russian agent!"
> You: "Huh."

(Boom. No debate. No drama. Just confusion.)

3. The Ghosting Method – Just Walk Away

Why it works:

- The best way to win is to not play the game.
- Arguing online drains your energy and accomplishes nothing.
- Let them rant into the void.

Best strategy:

- Type a full response.
- Delete it.
- Close your phone.
- Go enjoy your life.

KEY TAKEAWAYS

1. Social media arguments are unwinnable—don't try. (Arguing with a TDS sufferer online is like playing chess with a pigeon—it just knocks over the pieces and struts around like it won.)

2. TDS sufferers online thrive on outrage and attention. (They don't want debate. They want drama.)

3. Laughter disarms them faster than facts. (When you stop taking them seriously, they lose all power over you.)

4. The "Haha" react is your best friend. (It's the nuclear option without violating community guidelines!)

5. Your sanity is worth more than proving a stranger wrong. (Go outside. Touch grass. Enjoy life. Let them scream into their echo chamber.)

~

FINAL THOUGHTS

Social media was not built for rational discourse. It was built to keep people angry, engaged, and addicted to nonsense.

If you truly want to win against TDS sufferers online, there's only one strategy that works every time:

IGNORE THEM.

And if all else fails?

Log off and go enjoy your life.

Now, let's move on to "Chapter 7: Handling TDS in Your Relationship"—because if your spouse has TDS, things just got personal.

HANDLING TDS IN YOUR RELATIONSHIP

Finding love is hard enough in the modern world. Add Trump Derangement Syndrome into the mix, and suddenly, dating feels less like a romantic journey and more like walking through a minefield with clown shoes on.

Gone are the days when relationships were built on shared values, mutual respect, and a love for pizza and bad reality TV. Today, your ability to maintain a loving relationship could hinge on whether or not your significant other froths at the mouth when they hear "Trump 2024."

But fear not! Whether you're married, dating, or just swiping through Tinder, this chapter will help you navigate political insanity in your love life—without losing your sanity (or your spot on the couch).

What to Do if Your Spouse Has TDS

You love them. They love you. But there's just one problem —your spouse is a full-blown TDS sufferer.

Maybe they were normal before 2016 but have since developed a compulsion to yell at Fox News whenever they pass the TV. Maybe they can't get through a romantic dinner without blaming Trump for the price of eggs.

Whatever the case, you're here now, and you need a game plan.

Step 1: Don't Panic

First and foremost, take a deep breath.

Yes, your partner may be afflicted, but this is not a death sentence for your relationship. Unlike the people screaming in the streets after Election Day, you need to keep a level head.

Do not:

- Laugh in their face (tempting, but counterproductive).
- Ask them if they've considered therapy.
- Start playing Trump speeches in the background "accidentally."

Do:

- Remain calm.
- Resist the urge to debate every insane thing they say.
- Recognize that love > politics (if they do too).

- Because let's be real—if a relationship can survive a partner who doesn't refill the Brita filter, it can survive political differences.

Step 2: Find Common Ground (Movies, Food, NOT Politics)

There's a simple rule when you're dating someone with TDS:

Stick to what you both love, and avoid what makes them spiral into hysteria.

Safe zones:

- Food ("Wow, these nachos are amazing!" = No risk of political warfare.)
- Movies & TV ("What did you think of that new Netflix show?" = Still safe, unless it's *The Handmaid's Tale*.)
- Pets ("Look at the dog!" = Universal peace treaty.)
- Vacation Plans ("Let's go to the beach!" = No one fights about beaches.)

Danger zones:

- Late-night comedy shows (SNL is no longer comedy—it's a DNC press release.)
- Cable news (MSNBC is relationship poison.)
- "How was your day?" (Because somehow, they will find a way to blame Trump for it.)

Pro tip: If they start ranting about politics, hit them with a strategic distraction.

Example:

> Them: "You wouldn't BELIEVE what Trump did today—"
> You: "Wow, that reminds me—what should we get for dinner tonight?"

BOOM. Crisis averted.

Step 3: If Necessary, Implement a "No Politics" Rule at Home

Sometimes, the only way to preserve your sanity (and prevent your partner from rage-posting on Twitter at 1 AM) is to ban political talk in your household altogether.

The "No Politics" Rule:

- No MSNBC over breakfast.
- No political fights before bed.
- No impromptu lectures on "systemic oppression" when you're trying to enjoy football.

Think of it as a relationship safe zone—a place where love > partisanship.

If they resist? Remind them that:

- They don't need to be mad 24/7.

- Politics shouldn't dominate their happiness.
- You'd rather spend time cuddling, not arguing about tax policy.

Because if a relationship is just two people shouting CNN headlines at each other, what's even the point?

DATING WITH TDS IN THE MIX – RED FLAGS ON TINDER

Maybe you're still single and dipping your toes into the dating world. Congratulations! You're about to swipe through a minefield of political insanity.

Here are some red flags to watch for on Tinder, Bumble, and Hinge.

Red Flag #1: "If You Voted for Trump, Swipe Left."

Translation: "I value political purity over actual human connection."

If someone's first priority in a relationship is making sure you hate Trump as much as they do, imagine what the rest of your relationship will be like.

Spoiler: It won't be fun.

Red Flag #2: A Profile Full of Protest Photos

Translation: "I am perpetually angry, and you will hear about it daily."

If their profile pictures include:

- Holding a "Not My President" sign.
- Wearing a pink protest hat unironically.
- A dramatic selfie from a climate protest.

Run. Do not walk. ***RUN***.

Red Flag #3: If They Mention *The Handmaid's Tale* as a Documentary

Translation: "I believe we are one Trump away from women being forced into reproductive slavery."

Warning: Anyone who watches *The Handmaid's Tale* and genuinely believes it's a reflection of modern America is too far gone.

WHEN TO WALK AWAY VS. WHEN TO TRY GENTLE DEPROGRAMMING

Not every TDS sufferer is beyond saving. Some can be deprogrammed—but only if they're open to rational conversation.

Walk away if:

- They use "fascist" unironically.
- They cut off friends and family over politics.
- They believe Trump is controlling the weather.

In these cases? There is no cure. You cannot argue with someone who thinks *The Purge* is coming to real life.

Try deprogramming if:

- They can have a calm, rational discussion.
- They acknowledge that the media sometimes exaggerates.
- They don't hate you just for disagreeing.

If they meet these conditions, you can slowly introduce them to logic by:

- Asking questions instead of debating.
- Using humor instead of arguing.
- Avoiding direct confrontation (let them think they came to their own conclusions).

Example:

Them: "Trump is an evil dictator!"
You: "Wouldn't a dictator have, like, removed term limits and canceled elections?"

See? No argument—just gentle nudging toward reality.

KEY TAKEAWAYS

1. Relationships require mutual respect, not political purity tests. (You shouldn't have to pass a loyalty oath to date someone.)

2. Red flags on Tinder are real—pay attention. (Swipe left on political extremists—it's for your own good.)

3. A "No Politics" rule at home can save relationships. (No one wants to debate election integrity over morning coffee.)

4. Laughter is key to navigating political differences. (Humor disarms. Arguing just makes them double down.)

5. You can love someone without agreeing on everything. (If they love you more than they hate Trump, there's hope.)

∾

FINAL THOUGHTS

Political differences don't have to ruin relationships—but TDS can.

The key is balance, mutual respect, and a well-timed distraction technique.

And if all else fails?

Marry someone who doesn't yell at the TV.

Now, let's move on to "Chapter 8: Raising Kids in a World of TDS"—because if your child's teacher is telling them Trump is Voldemort, we have a problem.

8

RAISING KIDS IN A WORLD OF TDS

Parenting is tough enough as it is. You have to feed them, clothe them, and explain why they can't have ice cream for breakfast. But in today's world, you have an even greater challenge—raising a kid who can think for themselves in an era where their teachers, social media, and Disney+ are all telling them what to believe.

The biggest risk? TDS exposure at a young age.

- Your child's history teacher calls Trump the next Voldemort.
- Their school counselor hands out participation trophies while warning about "dangerous misinformation."
- Their science teacher spends more time discussing "social justice" than the periodic table.

You need a game plan to make sure your kid grows up informed, not indoctrinated—without getting yourself called into a meeting with the principal.

This chapter will teach you:

✔ How to explain political hysteria in kid-friendly terms.

✔ How to counter school indoctrination—without being labeled a domestic terrorist.

✔ How to raise a child who thinks critically and doesn't get swept up in mass hysteria.

Because let's be honest—your kid's sanity is more important than your PTA reputation.

How to Explain to Your Child Why Their Teacher Thinks Trump is Voldemort

At some point, your child will come home confused and ask, "Mom, why does my teacher say Trump is evil?"

This is a defining moment. You have two options:

- Option 1: Panic and yell, "WHAT ARE THEY TEACHING YOU?!" (Not ideal.)
- Option 2: Stay calm, smile, and teach your kid to think for themselves. (Winner.)

Step 1: Use Simple Terms

Kids don't need a full history lesson—just a simple, easy-to-understand explanation.

Try one of these:

> "Some people get really emotional about politics. They think if they don't like a president, it means the world is ending—but it's not."

> "Your teacher might have strong opinions, but that doesn't mean they're always right."

Warning: If your kid watches mainstream cartoons, they may already believe Trump is a villain.

- Paw Patrol: Normal kids show.
- Modern kids' shows: "Today, we'll learn about climate justice and how all rich people are evil!"

Be proactive—explain that stories, movies, and even teachers can be biased.

Step 2: Encourage Critical Thinking – Teach Them to Ask "Why?"

Kids are naturally curious. Instead of just telling them what to think, teach them to ask the right questions.

> "Why do some people think Trump is so bad?"

"Has the media ever exaggerated things before?"

"Do all leaders make mistakes? Or just the ones some people don't like?"

Key lesson: If a person can't explain their argument without getting emotional, they might not have a strong argument.

Step 3: Reassure Them – No, The World Isn't Ending

TDS sufferers thrive on fear. Kids should NOT inherit this anxiety.

If your child comes home terrified, thinking the country is doomed, remind them of these facts:

- America has survived far worse. (We made it through the Civil War, two World Wars, and disco—we'll be fine.)
- No president has absolute power. (We have checks and balances for a reason.)
- The news profits from fear. (Calm people don't stay glued to CNN.)

Example conversation:

"Mom, my teacher said Trump is destroying the country!"

- "Wow, that's a big claim. Did they explain how? Or just say that?"

- "Did they mention that the economy was doing well before COVID? Or that he helped negotiate peace deals?"
- "What do you think?

Pro tip: Turn their teacher's opinion into a debate exercise. Teach them that it's okay to question authority.

COUNTERING SCHOOL INDOCTRINATION WITHOUT GETTING CALLED TO THE PRINCIPAL'S OFFICE

Schools today are less about education and more about activism.

- Math class? Now includes discussions on "systemic oppression."
- English class? "Rewrite the Constitution to be more inclusive!"
- History class? Focused on why everything is America's fault.

You need a subtle strategy to keep your kid grounded—without becoming a target for the PTA's "Problematic Parents" list.

Step 1: Engage with Their Homework – Ask Questions Instead of Reacting

When your child brings home a ridiculous assignment, resist the urge to go full meltdown.

Bad Strategy: "This is propaganda! I'm calling the school board!"

Good Strategy: *"Hmm, this is interesting. What do YOU think about this?"

Example:

Assignment: Write about why capitalism is oppressive.

- Ask: "What do you think? Are there any good things about capitalism too?"
- Let them explore both sides—they'll learn more from that than from your anger.

Step 2: Encourage Them to Form Their Own Opinions

Most kids just repeat what they hear because they think they're supposed to.

The goal? Teach them that they're allowed to think for themselves.

- Encourage debate at home. Let them argue, question, and challenge ideas.
- Show them different sources. Compare news articles from different outlets so they see the bias.
- Teach them the phrase "I'm still thinking about it." It's okay to not have a strong opinion yet.

Key lesson: Just because everyone at school believes something doesn't make it true.

Step 3: Teach the Value of Free Speech

Many schools now push the idea that "offensive" speech should be banned.

Warning signs:

- Your kid says, "You shouldn't be allowed to say that!"
- Their school teaches that "words are violence."
- They think disagreeing with someone = hate speech.

Key lessons:

- Free speech exists to protect unpopular opinions.
- Nobody has the right to never be offended.
- The solution to bad ideas is more speech, not censorship.

Pro tip: If your kid starts sounding like a Twitter activist, remind them:

- Real debate is about logic, not feelings.
- If someone's argument is weak, shutting them up won't make it stronger.

TEACHING CRITICAL THINKING SO YOUR KID DOESN'T CATCH TDS

If you want to TDS-proof your child, teach them *how* to think, not *what* to think.

Teach Them to Research Both Sides

- Show them different news sources—let them compare how each one spins the same story.
- Teach them to ask: "What's the other side of this argument?"

Discuss Historical Perspective

- Remind them: "Politics has ALWAYS been dramatic."
- Every election is "the most important one of our lifetime" (until the next one).

Remind Them: The News Profits from Fear

- Calm people don't stay glued to the news.
- Fear = Ratings. Ratings = Money.

Key Takeaways

1. Schools often push one-sided narratives—be involved. (If you're not paying attention, someone else is shaping your child's worldview.)

2. Encourage critical thinking early. (A kid who asks "why" will never be brainwashed.)

3. Your kid's sanity is worth more than avoiding tough conversations. (It's better to teach them now than fix them later.)

4. Teach them media literacy—the news isn't always objective. ("Breaking News" is often just "Our Opinion, But Loud.")

5. Let them ask questions and form their own conclusions. (A kid who learns to think critically will never fall for mass hysteria.)

~

Final Thoughts

Raising kids today isn't just about keeping them fed and clothed—it's about protecting their minds from the insanity of the modern world.

The good news? You're their best defense.

Now, let's move on to "Chapter 9: The Media's Role in Spreading TDS"—because if we're going to talk about hysteria, we need to discuss the people profiting from it.

9

THE MEDIA'S ROLE IN SPREADING TDS

I f you ever wonder how perfectly reasonable people transformed into apocalyptic lunatics, you don't need to look much further than the mainstream media.

For years, networks like CNN, MSNBC, *The New York Times*, and *The Washington Post* engaged in what can only be described as psychological warfare—convincing ordinary Americans that Trump was not just a president they disagreed with, but an existential threat to human civilization.

They weren't just reporting the news. They were writing the script for a political horror movie, complete with daily episodes of mass hysteria, celebrity guest appearances, and the constant warning that we were mere moments away from descending into full-blown fascism.

The goal?

✔ Keep people scared.
✔ Keep people angry.
✔ Keep people glued to their screens.

Because in the media world, calm people don't tune in—but outraged people do.

THE GREAT GASLIGHTING – HOW THE MEDIA TURNED MILD LIBERALS INTO DOOMSDAY PREPPERS

If you want proof of how the media radicalized an entire demographic, just look at how they spun the exact same policies differently depending on who was in office.

Selective Outrage: Same Policies, Different Reaction

Under Obama:

✔ Border detention centers → "A necessary measure to handle immigration responsibly."
✔ Killing terrorists with drone strikes → "A tough but necessary decision for national security."
✔ Executive orders → "Bold leadership in times of gridlock."

Under Trump:

✖ Border detention centers → "Kids in cages! Literal concentration camps!"
✖ Killing terrorists with drone strikes → "An act of war that will destabilize the region!"

✖ Executive orders → "An authoritarian power grab!"

See the difference?

It wasn't about the policies—it was about the person implementing them.

This is how mild, common-sense liberals—people who once had nuanced political opinions—were turned into rabid, doomsday-obsessed extremists.

Apocalyptic Predictions That Never Happened

If you listened to the media during Trump's presidency, you would have believed that we were all about to die at any moment.

Some of their greatest hits included:

- "Trump will start World War III!" (Instead, he brokered peace deals in the Middle East.)
- "Trump is a Russian asset!" (Then he sanctioned Russia harder than Obama ever did.)
- "The economy will collapse!" (Then it hit record highs before COVID.)
- "Trump will never leave office!" (Then he... left office.)

Every alarmist headline was designed to provoke terror—and when none of it came true, did the media apologize?

Nope. They just moved on to the next manufactured crisis.

Rewriting History in Real-Time

One of the media's greatest tricks is their ability to flip the narrative overnight—counting on their audience to have the memory of a goldfish.

Example: The COVID Vaccine

- Under Trump: "I wouldn't trust a rushed vaccine!"
- Under Biden: "Take the vaccine immediately, or you're killing Grandma!"

Example: The Border Crisis

- Under Trump: "Children in cages! Human rights violation!"
- Under Biden: "Facilities for unaccompanied minors."

Example: Gas Prices

- Under Trump: "Presidents don't control gas prices!"
- Under Biden: "High gas prices? Trump's fault!"

If you ever feel like you're being gaslit by the news, you're not crazy—you're just paying attention.

THE TDS AMPLIFICATION CYCLE

Here's how the media keeps the outrage machine running:

Step 1: Invent an Outrage

Fabricate a scandal or twist something Trump said.
Example: "Trump called the military losers!"
(Never happened.)

Step 2: Spread It Like Wildfire

Twitter explodes within minutes.
Journalists write articles based on tweets, not facts.

Step 3: Celebrities and Influencers Jump In

Alyssa Milano tweets something insane.
The View dedicates an entire episode to crying about it.

Step 4: The Fact-Checkers Quietly Debunk It—Weeks Later

When no one is paying attention anymore, "Oops, turns out that story wasn't true."
No correction is given the same coverage as the original lie.

Step 5: Repeat Daily

The next fake scandal begins.
It's a never-ending cycle, designed to keep people angry and glued to the news.

Survival tip: Learn to recognize headlines designed to provoke TDS reactions.

The media knows exactly how to manipulate emotions—all they need is a well-crafted headline.

Here's how to decode them:

Experts warn that Trump's policies could lead to global catastrophe.
Translation: "Nothing happened, but we need clicks."

Sources say Trump said something racist behind closed doors.
Translation: "Zero proof, but trust us."

Democracy on the brink as Trump supporters breathe air.
Translation: "Stop thinking, just panic."

Key Takeaways

1. The media profits from outrage, not truth. (Calm people don't binge-watch CNN.)

2. TDS is fueled by headlines designed to provoke emotional reactions. (Rage = Ratings = Profit.)

3. "Anonymous sources" often mean "fiction." (If they had actual proof, they'd say it outright.)

4. Learn to spot media manipulation and filter out the nonsense. (If a story sounds too insane to be true... it probably is.)

5. Turn off the news and go touch some grass—it's good for your health. (Mental clarity begins when you unplug from the outrage machine.)

Suggested Resources

📖 *Unfreedom of the Press* – Mark Levin (Exposes media bias.)

📖 *Hoax* – Brian Stelter (Ironically, a book that became proof of media gaslighting.)

∿

Final Thoughts

The media isn't just reporting the news—they're manufacturing reality for a willing audience.

The only way to protect yourself from their manipulation?

Step back. Think critically. And remember that the real world is far more rational than the news makes it seem.

Now, let's move on to "Chapter 10: Can TDS Be Cured? (Or Are We Doomed?)"—because after everything we've learned, it's time to ask:

Can these people ever snap out of it?

Or are they too far gone?

10

CAN TDS BE CURED? (OR ARE WE DOOMED?)

After nine chapters of analyzing, diagnosing, and surviving Trump Derangement Syndrome, it's time to ask the big question:

Is recovery possible?

Can someone who once hyperventilated at the sight of a red hat ever return to normal society?

Or are they permanently lost, doomed to spend eternity doom-scrolling Twitter, ranting about "fascism," and believing that democracy hangs by a thread every time Trump orders a cheeseburger?

The answer is... complicated.

Some TDS sufferers eventually snap out of it—but not all.

This chapter will explore:

> ✔ Real-life examples of people who have recovered from TDS.
> ✔ What causes someone to "wake up" from political hysteria.
> ✔ How to deal with people who will never change.

Because not everyone is a lost cause—but some people definitely are.

CASE STUDIES OF TDS RECOVERY – YES, IT'S POSSIBLE!

TDS can be cured—but much like an intensive rehab program, it requires:

- Exposure to reality
- Breaking the cycle of media addiction
- Personal experiences that contradict the hysteria

Let's look at three groups of people who have successfully escaped the madness.

1. The Dave Rubin Effect

From Liberal Commentator to Media Skeptic

Dave Rubin was once a progressive darling. He worked for *The Young Turks*, the far-left YouTube channel that spends every day screeching about Republicans.

But then something interesting happened...

- He started asking questions.
- He noticed media hypocrisy.
- He realized that the people screaming about "tolerance" were actually the most intolerant.

Today? He's one of the loudest voices calling out media nonsense, and his show, *The Rubin Report,* is dedicated to free speech and independent thinking (Allen & Allen, 2021).

What happened?

✔ He stepped away from the left-wing echo chamber.
✔ He noticed the gaslighting in real-time.
✔ He had conversations with people outside his bubble.

Lesson: Some TDS sufferers wake up when they start thinking for themselves.

2. The WalkAway Movement

A Mass Exodus from Political Hysteria

The WalkAway Campaign was founded by Brandon Straka, a former liberal who realized he'd been lied to (Emmons, 2022).

At one point, he was a textbook TDS sufferer—believing that Trump was evil and that conservatives were all secretly plotting world domination.

Then... reality hit.

- He noticed that the media exaggerated everything.
- He started researching both sides.
- He saw Trump policies actually working.

He realized that the outrage machine was just that—a machine, designed to manipulate people.

And he wasn't alone. Thousands of people began posting their own stories about how they had "walked away" from the insanity.

Lesson: People who are exposed to both sides often realize that the truth is far more complicated than the media pretends.

3. The Independent Thinkers – People Who Took the Red Pill and Never Looked Back

Some people never had TDS to begin with, because they did something radical—they thought for themselves.

These are the people who:

- Read the news critically instead of accepting headlines at face value.
- Don't let emotions dictate their politics.

- Recognize that no president is the literal devil.

Many of these people were once liberals—but they started seeing through the nonsense.

And once you see it, you can't unsee it.

Lesson: The best way to avoid catching TDS is to never trust the media to do your thinking for you.

THE RED PILL MOMENT – WHAT CAUSES SOME TO WAKE UP?

Not everyone recovers from TDS, but those who do usually experience one of the following wake-up calls:

1. Seeing Media Lies Firsthand

Examples:

- They were told "Trump called Nazis 'very fine people.'"
- They actually watched the full speech and realized... that was a lie.
- Now they start questioning other things they've been told.

Lesson: Once people see one media lie, they start noticing all of them.

2. Personal Experience vs. The Narrative

Examples:

- They were told Trump's tax cuts only helped the rich.
- Then they looked at their own paycheck and saw their taxes actually went down.
- Suddenly, the media narrative isn't adding up.

Lesson: Reality always beats propaganda—but only if people pay attention.

3. Realizing Trump Wasn't Actually Hitler

Examples:

- They expected concentration camps and dictatorship.
- Instead, they saw record job growth, criminal justice reform, and peace deals.
- They waited for the fascism—but it never came.

Lesson: Some people wake up when they realize the world didn't end.

THE BEST WAY TO HANDLE TDS LONG-TERM

Even though some people can recover, many are too far gone.

You need to know how to handle them without wasting your sanity.

1. Know When to Walk Away

Some people won't change—and that's okay.

- If someone has based their entire personality on hating Trump, they won't let it go.
- You don't need to win every argument.
- Sometimes, the best move is to disengage.

2. Don't Waste Time Arguing with the Irrational

Key signs you should stop engaging:

- They use the word "fascist" incorrectly.
- They refuse to acknowledge reality.
- They respond emotionally instead of logically.

Lesson: Some people don't want the truth—they just want to stay angry.

3. Focus on Facts, Not Emotions

The best way to counter hysteria?

- Stay calm.
- Stick to facts.
- Let them expose their own irrationality.

When people rage and you stay cool, guess who looks like the sane one?

Lesson: Never let someone else's emotions dictate your logic.

Key Takeaways

1. TDS recovery is possible—but rare. (Most people stay lost in the outrage machine forever.)

2. Reality often contradicts the hysteria. (The truth is out there, but some people refuse to see it.)

3. Some people will never change—don't waste your energy. (Arguing with a fanatic is like arguing with a wall.)

4. Patience, humor, and strategic disengagement are key. (Stay sane by staying detached.)

5. The best cure? Step away from the media circus. (If you stop watching the hysteria, you stop feeling the hysteria.)

Suggested Resources

📖 *The Parasitic Mind* – Gad Saad (On how bad ideas infect society.)

📖 *Thinking, Fast and Slow* – Daniel Kahneman (Understanding cognitive biases.)

∾

Final Thoughts

So, can TDS be cured?

The short answer: Yes—but only for those willing to think for themselves.

For everyone else? They'll be screaming about "fascism" for years to come.

Your best bet?

Keep your sanity, laugh at the madness, and never argue with crazy.

~

FINAL WORDS

SANITY IS POSSIBLE – EVEN IN 2025

Y ou did it.

You've made it through *The Trump Derangement Syndrome Survival Guide* without losing your mind.

And now, as we stand in the aftermath of years of unhinged political hysteria, media gaslighting, and viral meltdowns, it's time to take a step back and ask:

Where do we go from here?

The answer is simple: We keep our sanity, keep our sense of humor, and refuse to be dragged into the endless cycle of outrage.

Because here's the truth:

- You are not alone. Millions of people see the madness for what it is.

- The media and politicians want you angry. But you don't have to play their game.
- Sanity is a choice. And in a world of hysterics, choosing to be sane is the ultimate act of rebellion.

So before we go, let's leave you with one last game plan for navigating the insanity—without letting it consume you.

You might sometimes feel like you're living in an alternate universe—where up is down, facts are offensive, and the phrase "two plus two equals four" is considered problematic.

It's easy to feel isolated.

It's easy to feel frustrated.

It's easy to wonder if you're the crazy one.

But you're not.

Millions of people see exactly what you see. The problem is, they're just as exhausted as you are.

So here's how you stay sane in a world gone mad:

1. Humor is Your Greatest Weapon

They say laughter is the best medicine, and when it comes to TDS, it's the only cure.

- Instead of getting mad, laugh at the absurdity.
- Instead of fighting online, send a meme.
- Instead of arguing with lunatics, enjoy the show.

Because once you stop taking them seriously, they lose all their power over you.

2. The Cycle Will Repeat – But You Can Rise Above It

Every election cycle, the media will say: "This is the most important election of our lifetime!"

Every time a Republican runs, they will be labeled a "threat to democracy."

Every minor political controversy will be "the end of America as we know it."

And yet...

America will survive.

The world won't end.

Life will go on.

Political hysteria is as old as time. The key to surviving it is recognizing the patterns—and choosing not to be part of the insanity.

Because at the end of the day...

Life is too short to be perpetually outraged.

3. Parting Wisdom: "You Can't Fix Crazy, But You Can Laugh About It"

If there's one lesson to take from this book, realize that:

- You can't fix your blue-haired cousin who thinks Trump is literally Voldemort.
- You can't fix your coworker who believes "democracy is over" because of tax cuts.
- You can't fix your friend who rage-posts about "fascism" while sipping a $7 Starbucks latte.

But you *CAN* laugh about it.

Because the moment you stop taking these people seriously, they lose all power over you.

And that's the secret to surviving TDS.

∾

Now, go forth, live your life, and always remember...

You can't fix crazy—but you CAN avoid it.

BONUS

A TDS RECOVERY PLAN FOR THOSE WHO WANT TO HELP THEIR FRIENDS ESCAPE THE MADNESS

Some people are too far gone.

Others?

They just need a push in the right direction.

If you have a TDS-afflicted friend or family member who *might* be open to reality, here's a gentle deprogramming strategy:

Step 1: Limit Their Media Intake – Help Them Detox from CNN

- CNN, MSNBC, *The New York Times*—these are the oxygen supply for TDS.
- If they can step away from the outrage machine, they might start thinking for themselves.
- Encourage them to take a break. Suggest a news detox. See what happens.

Step 2: Encourage Critical Thinking – Ask "Why Do You Believe That?"

The key to breaking free from TDS is questioning everything.

If they say "Trump is a dictator!", don't argue—just ask:

- "How exactly is he a dictator?"
- "Which freedoms did he take away?"
- "How does a dictator get impeached twice?"

By simply forcing them to explain their logic, you plant a seed of doubt.

Step 3: Expose Them to Alternative Viewpoints – But Do It Subtly

Do not say, "Here, read this conservative article!" (They'll reject it immediately.)

Do say:

- "Hey, this article had an interesting take—I'd love to hear your thoughts."
- "I saw this interview and thought you'd find it interesting."

The key is not to push—just to plant the idea that other perspectives exist.

Step 4: Use Humor as a Bridge – Laugh First, Debate Second

Humor is the ultimate deprogramming tool.

- People get defensive when they feel attacked.
- They lower their guard when they're laughing.

Instead of debating:

- Send a *Babylon Bee* article that mocks media hysteria.
- Share a funny meme about political overreaction.
- Watch a comedic take on the absurdity of the news cycle.

Once they start laughing at the craziness, they're one step closer to waking up.

Step 5: Know When to Let Go – Some People Are Too Far Gone

Some people WANT to be angry.

Some people are addicted to the outrage.

Some people will NEVER admit they were wrong.

For those people? Let. Them. Go.

- You can't argue someone out of a delusion they're emotionally invested in.

- You can't help someone who doesn't want to wake up.
- You can't change someone's mind if they don't want it changed.

And that's okay.

Your peace of mind is more important than proving a point.

KEY TAKEAWAYS

1. Political hysteria is temporary—sanity is forever. (Elections come and go, but common sense is eternal.)

2. The best way to win is to stop playing their game. (Don't engage in unwinnable arguments. Just live your life.)

3. You can't control others, but you can control how you react. (Let them scream. You go enjoy a steak and a peaceful evening.)

4. Live your life—don't let politics consume you. (There's more to life than Twitter meltdowns and cable news panic attacks.)

5. If all else fails, buy this book for your TDS-afflicted friends. (Maybe, just maybe, they'll read it and snap out of it.)

∼

FINAL THOUGHTS

Go forth and be sane.

Congratulations. You've survived the insanity.

Now, it's time to go forth and live your life—unbothered, untriggered, and completely free from the chains of political hysteria.

And remember:

You can't fix crazy. But you CAN enjoy the show.

Now go touch some grass. It's good for you.

SPECIAL REQUEST

A FRIENDLY (AND FUNNY) REMINDER TO LEAVE A REVIEW!

Congratulations! You've just survived *The Trump Derangement Syndrome Survival Guide* with your mental stability intact—a true feat in today's world.

Now, I have one small favor to ask...

PLEASE LEAVE A REVIEW!

Why? Because if this book goes viral (fingers crossed), you can bet your last non-inflated dollar that a horde of angry, blue-haired keyboard warriors will storm Amazon to leave 1-star reviews out of pure emotional distress.

Did you laugh? *Leave a review.*

Did this book help you survive a family dinner? *Leave a review.*

Did you successfully use the "Nod and Smile Method" at work? *Leave a review.*

Did you enjoy watching the inevitable meltdown this book will cause in the reviews section? (You know what to do.)

Remember: Your review is more than just feedback—it's a counterattack against the professionally outraged.

So take a moment, help an author out, and leave your honest (but hopefully not deranged) review.

And if you really loved the book? Buy an extra copy for your TDS-afflicted friend. It won't cure them... but at least you'll get to enjoy the reaction.

Thanks for your support—now go forth and enjoy your sanity!

https://amzn.to/43AFGfU

RESOURCES

Allen, V., & Allen, V. (2021, July 2). Why Talk show host Dave Rubin walked away from left. The Daily Signal. https://www.dailysignal.com/2021/06/11/why-talk-show-host-dave-rubin-walked-away-from-left/

Emmons, L. (2022, September 2). PROFILE: #WalkAway founder Brandon Straka discusses his political journey. The Post Millennial. https://thepostmillennial.com/profile-walkaway-activist-brandon-straka-discusses-his-political-journey/

MSEd, K. C. (2025, January 27). Cognitive dissonance and the discomfort of holding conflicting beliefs. Verywell Mind. https://www.verywellmind.com/what-is-cognitive-dissonance-2795012

ABOUT THE AUTHOR

LLOYD BECKMAN

Lloyd Beckman is a writer, satirist, and political observer who has spent years watching the world lose its mind—one meltdown at a time. Armed with sharp wit and a refusal to take political hysteria seriously, he has made it his mission to help sane people survive in an age of outrage and media-driven panic.

When he's not dissecting the latest social media firestorm, Lloyd enjoys strong coffee, bad political debates, and watching Twitter mobs self-destruct in real-time.

The Trump Derangement Syndrome Handbook is his definitive guide to navigating the madness—because if we can't stop the insanity, we might as well laugh at it.